ANCIENT EGYPT

by Robert Nicholson and Claire Watts

Editorial Consultant: George Hart M.Phil,
Education Department, British Museum

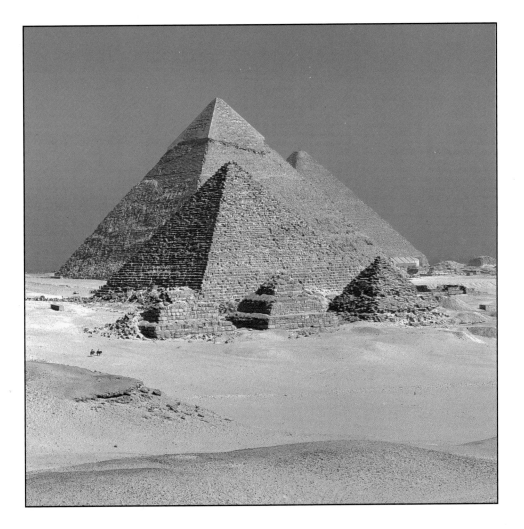

TWO-CAN

First published in Great Britain in 1991 by
Two-Can Publishing Ltd
346 Old Street
London EC1V 9NQ

© Two-Can Publishing Ltd, 1991
Text © Robert Nicholson, 1991
Design by Millions Design

Printed and bound in Hong Kong

This impression published in 1991 in association with
Scholastic Publications Ltd.

4 6 8 10 9 7 5 3

British Library Cataloguing in Publication Data

Nicholson, Robert
Ancient Egypt
    1. Egypt, ancient period
    I. Title II. Watts, Claire
    932
    ISBN: 1-85434-057-3

Photographic credits:
Werner Forman Archive: p.5, p.17(l), p.19(b), p.21(b), p.22, p.24(r), p.30(l);
Sonia Halliday: p.6; Michael Holford: p.1, p.6, p.10, p.11(t), p.12, p.13,
p.15, p.16, p.19(t), p.21(t), p.23, p.24(l), p.30(r); Ronald Sheridan: p.11(l),
p.17(r), p.20, p.21(c).

Illustration credits:
Jon Davis (Linden Artists): p.4, p.8, p.11, p.13, p.14, p.15, p.16,
p.18, p.19, p.20, p.22, p.23, p.24, p.31
Maxine Hamil: cover, pp.25-29

Contents

All words marked in **bold** can be found in the glossary.

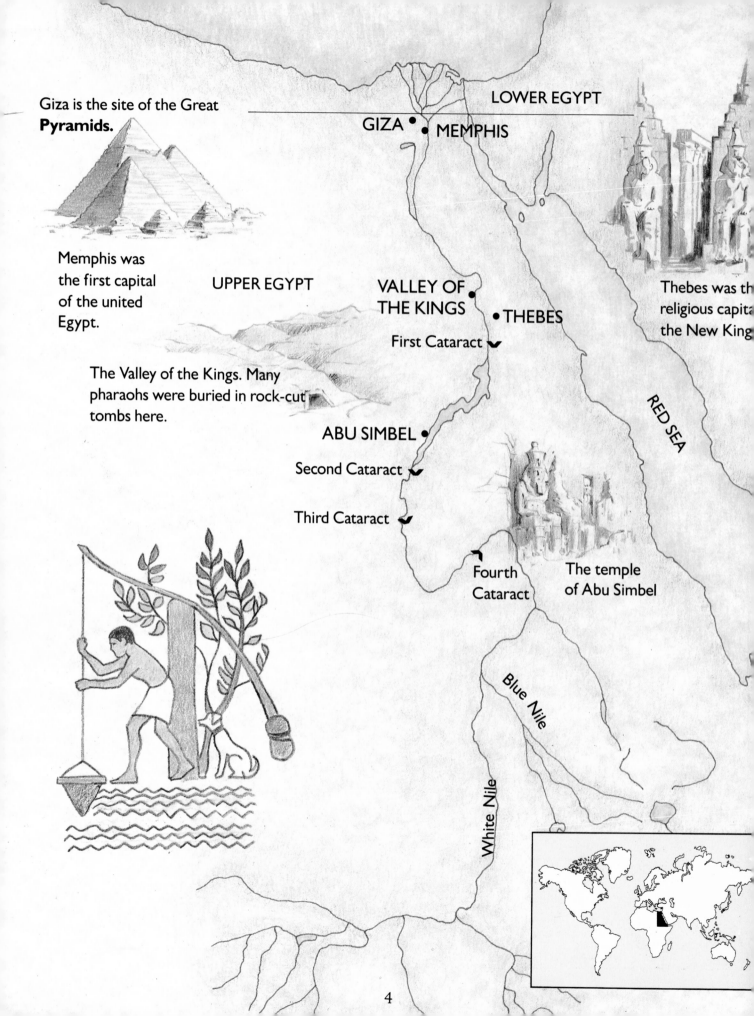

Giza is the site of the Great **Pyramids.**

LOWER EGYPT

GIZA ● ● MEMPHIS

Memphis was the first capital of the united Egypt.

UPPER EGYPT

VALLEY OF THE KINGS ●

● THEBES

First Cataract ⌄

The Valley of the Kings. Many pharaohs were buried in rock-cut tombs here.

ABU SIMBEL ●

Second Cataract ⌄

Third Cataract ⌄

Fourth Cataract

The temple of Abu Simbel

Thebes was th[e] religious capit[al] the New King[dom]

RED SEA

Blue Nile

White Nile

4

The Egyptian World

The great **civilisation** of ancient Egypt began over 5,000 years ago, when Menes, the ruler of Upper Egypt, overcame Lower Egypt and united the two kingdoms. The Egyptians never forgot that Egypt had once been two lands, and the **pharaoh** was known as *king of Upper and Lower Egypt.*

For the next 3,000 years Egypt remained strong and powerful and gradually expanded to take over new lands. The Egyptians were a sophisticated people who developed architecture and new efficient methods of government and made important discoveries in medicine and astronomy.

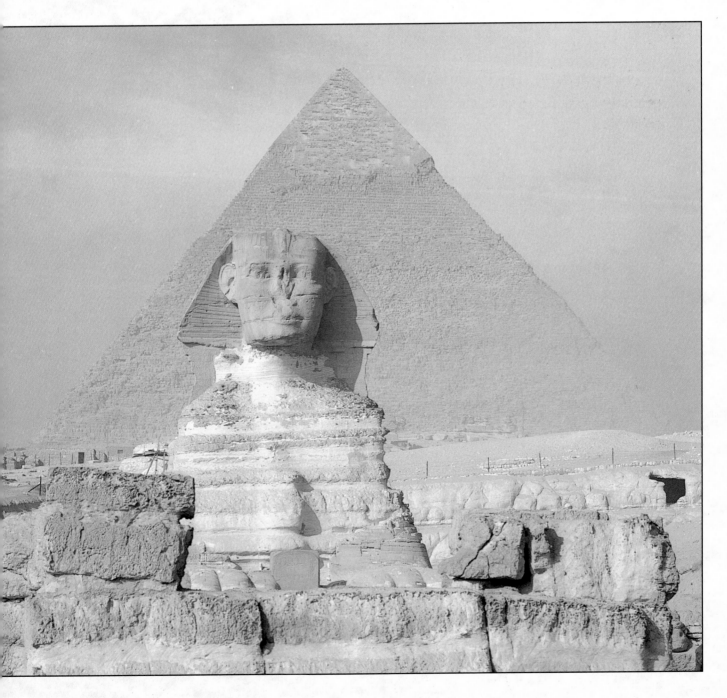

The Gift of the Nile

Egypt is a long, thin country running along the length of the Nile, an oasis surrounded by desert. A Greek arriving in Egypt for the first time called the country *the gift of the Nile*, because it was the Nile which provided most of Egypt's wealth. The rest of Egypt is barren and rocky with little water.

This desert, which the ancient Egyptians called *the Red Land*, cannot support much life, although precious stones and metals are found there. Once a year the **Akhet** or **Inundation** came, flooding the river valley from July to September and leaving behind rich, fertile black mud, *the Black Land*. The amount of water brought by the floods was critical: too little meant that the crops would fail and there would be famine, too much and houses, livestock and people would be swept away by the river. For this reason, the water level was

constantly checked with a measure known as a **nilometer**, and the changing seasons were carefully monitored to try to prevent famine. In order to read the seasons the Egyptians studied the cycle of the Sun, the Moon and the stars, which led them to divide the year up into 365 days, made up of 12 months each with 30 days and 5 extra days.

◀ The Egyptians also depended on the Nile for transport. They did not usually use carts with wheels, as these were useless in the desert sands or in the mud. Heavy loads were dragged to and from river barges on rollers or sledges.

▼ The green and fertile land around the Nile stands out against the barren desert that surrounds it.

The Pharaoh

The pharaoh of Egypt was an absolute ruler, answerable to no-one. Whatever he decided was the law. In fact one way to say *justice* was "what the pharaoh loves" and to say *wrong-doing* was "what the pharaoh hates".

The pharaoh was considered to be a god. He married his own sister or half-sister so that his children would have the blood of the gods. He often had many other wives too. His subjects treated him with all the reverence they gave to their other gods, kneeling before him with their foreheads touching the ground. As a sign of respect they never referred to him by his own name, but used official names instead. One of these was *great house* or *per-ao*, which is where our word pharaoh comes from.

A complex administrative system was set up to deal with the governing of the five million people in the empire. The pharaoh's chief adviser or **vizier** was the second most powerful man in the kingdom, standing in for the pharaoh and deciding what matters were important enough for the pharaoh's ears. Under the vizier's rule were numerous local governors called **nomarchs** who were each in charge of a region or nome. They ensured that everyone paid their taxes, which were in the form of goods or services as the Egyptians did not use money.

▼ With all the different religious and administrative obligations upon him, the pharaoh had very little time to himself.

Famous Pharaohs

In the 3,000 years when Egypt was powerful there were over 300 pharaohs. Some were great warriors and some helped to establish the strong government of Egypt, but we know very little about most of them apart from their names.

Tutankhamen

Tutankhamen was just a boy when he became pharaoh. His reign lasted for only ten years but he restored order to the country after the previous pharaoh, Akenaten, had caused chaos by trying to introduce a new religion. Tutankhamen started building a number of huge temples to honour the god Amun-Re.

Tuthmosis III

Tuthmosis, the greatest of the warrior pharaohs, conquered Palestine and Syria and never lost a battle.

Cleopatra VII

Cleopatra was one of the few women to become pharaoh in her own right. She tried to form a political alliance with the Roman empire, first through **Julius Caesar** and then by marrying **Mark Antony**. After a huge military defeat she killed herself.

Gods and Temples

Religion was a very important part of Egyptian life. There were gods to deal with every imaginable event or problem. These gods often took on the shape or part of the shape of a particular animal. For example Bast, the goddess of joy and love, was usually shown as a cat and Anubis, the god who protected the tombs of the dead, was shown either as a jackal or a man with a jackal's head.

Each god had a temple where people could come to worship and ask favours. A statue of the god stood in a room at the back of the temple. It was only brought out on feast days and even then the statue itself was kept hidden inside a shrine. Ordinary people could only go as far as the entrance hall of the temple, where they would meet the god's servant, the priest. The priest would take messages and offerings from the people and interpret the god's answers. Often the animals associated with the god were kept in the temple.

The temple was considered to be the home of the god. Each day meals were laid before his statue for the god to eat if he chose. Later the food was removed and eaten by the priests.

▼ The temple of Amun at Karnak was extended by pharaoh after pharaoh until it was the size of six huge cathedrals.

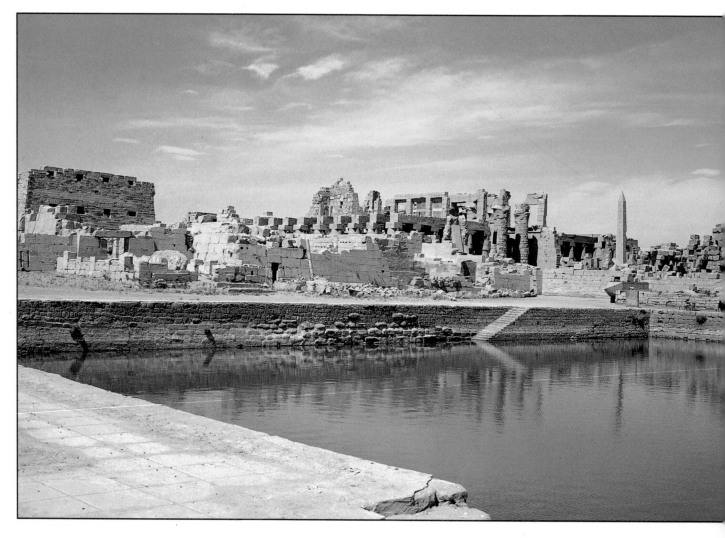

10

Important Gods

RE was the sun god. He took on different shapes at different times of the day.

AMUN was the god of the air and of Thebes. His name means *hidden*. When Thebes became the capital of Egypt, he merged with Re to become the chief god, Amun-Re.

OSIRIS was the god of the dead, who judged all men when they died.

ISIS was the sister-wife of Osiris and the goddess and protector of women.

AMUN   OSIRIS   ISIS

▶ This wall-painting shows Hathor, goddess of music and love, in the form of a cow.

▲ The Jackal was sacred to Anubis, god of the dead.

The Afterlife

The Egyptians believed firmly that with proper preparation a person could live again after death. This preparation involved preserving the body of the dead person and providing it with all the food, furniture, tools and riches which it was thought would be needed in the afterlife. Even the poorest people were buried with scraps of food.

Journey to the Afterlife

The dead person had to make a long and hazardous journey before he could enjoy the pleasures of the afterlife. He had to pass a giant serpent and a crocodile, avoid being caught in fishing nets and a fiery furnace, and escape from people trying to drown him and chop his head off.

When the dead man reached the underworld, the god Anubis measured his heart against the Feather of Truth. If they balanced, he would be greeted by Osiris, but if not, he would be devoured by a monster which was part-crocodile, part-lion and part-hippopotamus.

▼ In this painting Anubis weighs the heart of the dead person, while Osiris waits to greet him. Thoth, god of wisdom, records what is happening. Which do you think is the dead person? Can you find the eleven judges?

Mummies

The body of a dead person was preserved by a complicated embalming process known as **mummification.**

First the intestines, stomach, liver and lungs were removed from the body. All were put in jars and placed under the protection of four gods. The body was then covered with a salt called natron to dry it.

After 40 days the body was packed with linen, sawdust and spices and finally wrapped in linen bandages soaked in resin. Magic charms and scraps of linen with spells written on them were placed between the layers of bandages. This took 30 days.

The mummy was placed in a coffin of wood, clay or stone.

The Pyramids

The tombs of the pharaohs were huge and elaborate and took many years to build. The pyramids were the tombs of some of the early pharaohs. Such were the riches inside that tomb-robbing became very common, and later pharaohs had maze-like tombs hidden underground. Most of these were eventually discovered by tomb robbers.

Each of the blocks of stone used to build the pyramid had to be hauled into place by hand. Ramps of packed earth were built first to move the stone up to the level where it was needed.

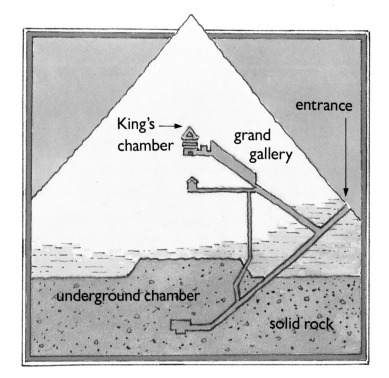

▲ Inside the Great Pyramid.

▼ The Great Pyramid at Giza was originally 147m tall. It contained over two million blocks of stone, each weighing about 2.5 tonnes, although some of them weighed up to 14 tonnes. It was covered in highly polished limestone which gleamed in the Sun. It took 50,000 people 20 years to build.

▲ Large blocks of stone could be lifted using wooden wedges.

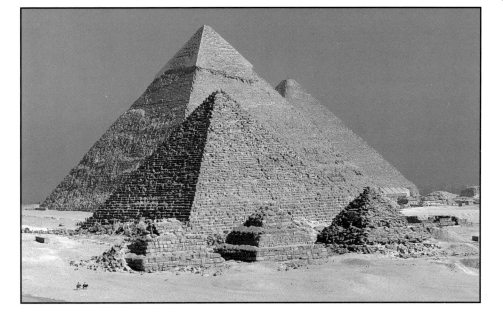

Writing and Education

Early Egyptians wrote using picture letters called **hieroglyphs**. There were over 700 of these letters, some of which stood for whole words. The word signs were simple pictures illustrating an object or action. For example, a series of wavy lines were drawn to mean water. Other signs stood for one or two letters. There were no vowels in the alphabet, but the Egyptians managed quite well without them. Try writing in English with no vowels – you should still find it quite easy to read.

Gradually hieroglyphs became less detailed to make them quicker and easier to write. This form of writing was used by scribes for everyday documents, such as records of taxes. Hieroglyphs were still used for writing on tombs and monuments.

The Egyptians did not use paper but wrote on **papyrus**, made from reed stems which had been flattened, dried and stuck together to make pages. A thin, sharpened reed dipped in ink was used to write with.

▲ Many paintings in tombs include writing that explains what is happening in the picture.

Learning

Most people could not read or write. Children were usually taught a trade or craft by their parents. There were some schools where boys training to be scribes were taught writing, mathematics and astronomy. They learnt to read and write by copying and chanting wisdom texts which gave advice on morals and behaviour. These schools cannot have been very pleasant places to be, as the children were regularly beaten. One scribe wrote "the ears of a boy are in his back. He listens only when he is beaten".

| ♀ = life | = hawk | = stone | = shape |

▲ Here are some hieroglyphs with their English meanings. Can you spot any of these symbols in the picture below?

▲ A scribe's ink palette and brushes made from reeds.

◄ Scribes sat cross-legged with their writing materials on their laps.

At Home

Egyptian houses were clustered together on the higher ground at the edge of the river's flood area. They were built of sun-baked brick made from mud and straw. In Egypt's hot, dry climate these bricks lasted a long time. Only buildings which were expected to last for eternity, like temples and tombs, were built of stone.

Houses were very plain, square buildings. They were often surrounded by a wall and had steps outside leading to a flat roof. Inside, the house was dark because of the tiny windows.

The front room of an ordinary house was used by the man of the family to conduct his trade. Sometimes people even kept livestock in this room. There was little furniture in the houses of ordinary people, just a chest for clothes, and storage jars for food.

The second room was usually large with windows high up in the walls. This was used for receiving guests and eating meals. The kitchen, bathroom and bedrooms were at the back of the house.

Sometimes cooking was done on the flat roofs of the houses to avoid the risk of fire.

The houses of the rich looked similar to ordinary houses from the outside, although they were larger. Inside they were decorated with wall paintings and panelling, where they were protected from the cutting desert winds.

Furniture Facts

● The Egyptians used little furniture. Poor people usually had none, and even the rich often sat on the floor.

● Much of the furniture was portable, like this folding wooden stool (right), which would have had a leather seat.

● Beds, like most furniture, were made from wood and reeds. Wooden head-rests were used instead of pillows.

Work and Play

Work

Most Egyptians were farmers but some had
other jobs. As well as priests, scribes and
government officials, there were all sorts of
craftsmen. Building projects like the pyramids
required hundreds of skilled men:
draughtsmen to design the structure, masons
to carve the stone, painters to decorate the
walls, sculptors to carve the statues and other
craftsmen to make all the furniture, jewellery,
tools and utensils which were to be put inside.

As the Egyptians did not use money, the
craftsmen were paid with food, drink, clothes
and lodging. Sometimes the men working on
royal tombs went on strike if their payment did
not turn up.

▶ Egyptian craftsmen used tools made from wood,
bronze and other metals.

Play

Egyptians worked very hard – sometimes for eight days in a row, followed by two days off. They spent much of their spare time very actively: hunting, dancing and playing athletic games like wrestling, ball games and acrobatics. Rich people held sumptuous dinner parties, where guests were entertained by acrobats and musicians.

Board games were popular and **senet** was the favourite. It was played on a board divided into three rows of ten squares. Each player had seven pieces and the aim was to get all your pieces to the end of the board, whilst preventing your opponent from doing the same.

Children played with wooden balls and tops as well as dolls and carved wooden animals.

▲ Some Egyptian toys had moving parts. This cat's jaw is operated with a string, and the wooden horse moves along on its wheels.

► This senet board has a little drawer to keep the pieces in when they are not being used.

▼ Do you know what games these children are playing?

Food

The fertile soil around the Nile helped produce a wide variety of crops for the Egyptian people. There was a plentiful supply of wheat and barley for bread and beer. Vegetables such as onions, leeks, lettuce and all kinds of beans were eaten in great quantities. They were often served with an oil and vinegar dressing, rather like modern salad dressing. There was less fruit because it was harder to grow in the extremes of the Egyptian climate. However, the Egyptians did manage to grow figs, dates and pomegranates, and grapes to make wine.

People did not eat a great deal of meat. Cattle were more often kept as beasts of burden and for milk than for meat. Feasts for the rich included a wide variety of meats though, including such strange delicacies as antelope and hyena. Fish was eaten mostly by the poor.

The Egyptians ate from low tables seated on the floor. They used their fingers to eat with. The pharaoh had a servant to wash his hands between each course.

Egyptian Bread

Try making your own Egyptian bread. You can add chopped dates to the dough if you like.

You will need:
400 g wholemeal flour
225 ml water
½ tsp salt

- Add the water to the flour and salt quite slowly, mixing thoroughly.
- Knead the dough.
- Shape into small rounds or triangles.
- Cover with a cloth and leave overnight.
- Bake for 30 minutes at 180°C.

Mix up the ingredients.

Knead the dough.

Cover the dough overnight before baking.

Farming Facts

● There were three seasons in the farming year: the Inundation (June – October), the Emergence (November – January) when the floodwaters subsided, and the Drought (February – June).

● Each farmer's land was marked by heavy stones which could not be moved by the floods.

● A complex irrigation system allowed flood water to be stored in huge reservoirs so that it could be used when needed.

● During the Inundation, when little farmwork could be done, many people worked on the pharaoh's building projects as a way of paying their taxes.

▲ Egyptian farmers used wooden ploughs drawn by oxen.

Clothes

The clothes worn by most Egyptian people were made from linen. Flax, which linen is made from, grows well in the Egyptian climate, and the fabric is cool and comfortable. Most people wore undyed linen, decorated by pleating. Only the rich could afford brightly coloured cloth.

Men wore a length of linen wrapped around their waists like a kilt or a simple tunic. Labourers usually wore linen loincloths or nothing at all. Men were usually clean-shaven or had small, pointed beards.

Women wore ankle-length dresses, often with one or both shoulders bare.

Most children wore no clothes and had their heads shaved, except for a long plait on the right side of their head which was called "the lock of youth". In cold weather everyone except the priests wore cloaks of wool or animal skins. Sandals were made from reeds or leather, with a strap over the instep and between the first and second toes.

▲ Egyptian mirrors were made of bronze, and combs of ivory or wood.

Egyptian Cosmetics

● Personal appearance was very important to the Egyptians. They used perfumed oils to keep their skin healthy in the harsh desert winds.

● Rich Egyptian men and women wore wigs made from a mixture of real hair and vegetable fibres. The strands were fixed to a netting base with wax.

● Men and women wore eye make-up to protect their eyes from sand and dust.

● At dinner parties guests and servants wore cones of perfumed oil on their heads. The perfume gradually melted and ran down their hair and clothes.

Nut's Children

The ancient Egyptians told many stories about their gods and about the world around them. Often these stories would try to explain something that the people did not really understand. Nut's Children tries to explain why the Moon waxes and wanes.

n long ago times, Re, the chief of all the gods, till reigned on Earth as a living pharaoh. He ved in a huge palace on the banks of the Nile, nd all the people of Egypt came to bow down efore him. All his courtiers did exactly what e asked, and he spent his time hunting, laying games and feasting. It was a vonderful life!

However, one day a courtier came to him nd told him about a conversation he had verheard. Thoth, god of wisdom and magic, ad told the goddess Nut that one day her son vould be Pharaoh of Egypt.

Re was furious. How could anyone but he ossibly be Pharaoh? No-one else was worthy f the task, and besides, he had no intention of ever giving up the throne. He raged about in his chambers, shouting at the top of his voice.

"How dare they suggest such a thing! Why, they are probably plotting to get rid of me at this very moment. But no child of Nut will de-throne me!"

He thought and thought about a way to protect his throne. Eventually, summoning all the magic powers he possessed, he spoke these words: "I lay this curse upon her: no child of Nut will be born on any day or any night of any year."

News travelled quickly amongst the gods, so Nut soon heard of Re's curse. She was quite heart-broken. She badly wanted a child, but she knew that Re's magic was very strong. How could she break the curse? The only person who might be able to help her was Thoth, wisest of all gods, so she set off to see him at once.

Thoth loved Nut dearly and, when he saw her tears, he decided at once to do all he could to help her.

"I cannot lift Re's curse," he said, "but I may be able to get round it. Just wait here."

Thoth knew that Khonsu, the Moon god, was a great gambler, so he went to visit him and challenged him to a game of senet.

Khonsu did not stop to think for a moment. He could not resist the challenge.

"O, Thoth," he said. "You may be the wisest of all the gods, but I am the greatest senet player there has ever been. I have never lost a game. I will certainly play you and I will win every game easily!"

The two sat down to play. From the very start, Thoth won every game. All seven of his pieces seemed to reach the far end of the board before Khonsu's pieces had even moved.

"You have just been lucky up till now, Thoth," said Khonsu. "I wager an hour of my light that I will win the next game."

But still he lost! Thoth kept on winning and Khonsu kept on wagering his own light until Thoth had won enough of Khonsu's light to make up five whole days. Then Thoth stood up, thanked Khonsu for the game and left, taking Khonsu's light with him.

"What a coward," muttered Khonsu to himself. "My luck was just starting to change. I would certainly have won the next game!"

Thoth fitted the five extra days in between the end of that year and the beginning of the next. Until that time the year had been made up of twelve months, each with 30 days, making a total of 360 days in the year. That number remained the same, but the five extra days set the calendar right.

Nut was overjoyed when Thoth told her what he had done. Because the five extra days were not days in any year, Nut's children could be born on these days without breaking Re's curse. On the first day Nut gave birth to Osiris, who was to be Pharaoh after Re; on the second day to Harmachis, who is immortalised as the Sphinx; on the third day Set, who later killed Osiris and became Pharaoh for a while; on the fourth day Isis, who was to be the wife of Osiris, and on the fifth day Nephthys, who was to be Set's wife.

As for Khonsu the Moon god, he was so weakened after the game with Thoth that he lost much of his strength for ever. He could no longer shine brightly all the time. Even today the Moon only shines brightly on a few days of the month and has to spend the rest of the time gathering its strength together.

How We Know

Have you ever wondered how we know so much about the lives of the ancient Egyptians, although they lived thousands of years ago?

Evidence from the Ground

Archaeologists have found many objects which were thrown away by ancient Egyptians and which have been preserved by the hot, dry climate of Egypt. They have also built up a very clear picture of everyday life from the objects found in tombs and the paintings on the walls.

▲ Tomb-paintings like this one give a detailed picture of life in ancient Egypt.

Evidence around Us

Many people in Egypt today have a lifestyle similar to that of the ancient Egyptians of thousands of years ago. Farmers on the banks of the Nile still live in houses built of sun-baked brick, following the same pattern as the ancient houses, and certain farming methods are the same. A huge dam built on the Nile now controls the flooding of the river and makes people's lives much easier.

Evidence from Books

The Egyptians were great writers. Scribes recorded everything that happened in minute detail, and many of these records survive today. It is thanks to them that we know more about the Egyptians than we do about many peoples who have lived since them.

▲ It was not until 1822, some time after the **Rosetta Stone** had been discovered, that Egyptian texts could be read. The same text was written on it in hieroglyphs, an Egyptian script called **demotic** and Greek. A Frenchman called Campolian used this and other monuments to find the key to hieroglyphs.

Glossary

absolute ruler
a ruler who can make laws without consulting any other person or group of people.

Akhet
the yearly flooding season on the Nile. (Egyptian word)

Caesar, Julius
Roman general who became leader of the Roman empire.

civilisation
an organised society which has developed social customs, government, technology and the arts.

demotic
form of ancient Egyptian writing developed from 700 BC onwards used for business and administration.

hieroglyph
symbol standing for a word or group of letters used in ancient Egyptian writing.

inundation
the yearly flooding of the Nile valley.

Mark Antony
Roman general who married Cleopatra.

mummification
process of drying and embalming by which a body is preserved.

nilometer
a measure used to check the water level of the Nile.

nomarch
official in charge of the running of a region or nome.

papyrus
type of paper made out of flattened reed stems.

pharaoh
the ruler of ancient Egypt.

pyramid
tomb with four triangular sides built for the early Egyptian pharaohs.

Rosetta Stone
a carved stone which gave a major clue to the deciphering of hieroglyphs. It was found by a French officer in 1799.

senet
a game played by the Egyptians with a board and counters.

vizier
chief adviser to the pharaoh. At times there were two of them.

Index

For more information about TWO-CAN books, write to TWO-CAN Publishing, 346 Old Street, London, EC1V 9NQ.